Shirts & Blouses

SIMPLE DRESSMAKING 1

Maureen Goldsworthy

Mills & Boon Ltd
London Sydney Toronto

I am most grateful to Rosamund Keer and my daughter Alice Helps who modelled the blouses. I should also like to thank Robert Saunders of Wright Photography for the photographs, taken at Warwick Castle by kind permission of Warwick Castle Ltd.

For P.O.G.

First published in 1980

© Maureen Goldsworthy 1980

ISBN 0 263 06425 5

Designed by Richard Brown Associates

Printed in Great Britain by
Fletcher & Son Ltd, Norwich
and bound by
Richard Clay (The Chaucer Press) Ltd,
Bungay, Suffolk

for the publishers Mills & Boon Ltd,
15–16 Brooks Mews,
London W1Y 1LF

CONTENTS

INTRODUCTION

This book contains all the information you need to make a perfectly-fitting blouse in any design you wish, from a classic shirt to a pleated or gathered style, with any type of sleeve or collar.

The first section shows show to draft the basic block patterns from your own measurement chart. The next part of the book shows how to translate these blocks into a working pattern for the design you have chosen. The last section gives full instructions for making up the blouse.

The disadvantage of using a commercial pattern – apart from the price – is that it will be in a stock size while you may not be. You are then faced with having to alter the pattern. But by drafting your personal blocks, based on no fewer than ten of your own measurements, an exact fit is ensured at every point. All your future blouse patterns of whatever style are derived from the permanent record of the blocks.

None of this is difficult, though to begin with it does take a little time. You will probably need two or three hours to draft the blocks, then another two or three to make the final pattern with all the styling details. But if you can follow an ordinary dressmaking pattern, you should have no trouble with these instructions. The system of drafting used here will give you an accurate fit: that is the most important point. But it is also a much simpler system than most, because the blocks have been planned just for the shape of a single type of garment – the blouse.

Paper

Squared dressmaker's paper may be difficult to find and is expensive. It is much better to use a roll of ceiling lining paper. This is strong, easily obtainable and quite wide enough. Besides, you will need plenty of it and it is cheap.

Thin card

This is obtainable from art stationers. Three sheets will be needed for the final pattern blocks.

Set square

This is handy but not essential. Without one, lines at exact right angles to the edge of the paper can be made by creasing. When you fold across the width of the paper keep the side edges exactly level with each other; the creases will then be at right angles to the side edges (*Figure 1*).

Tracing wheel

A wheel with sharp metal points used to transfer pattern outlines from an upper to a lower sheet of paper (*Figure 2*). Obtainable from haberdashery (US notions) departments. A plastic wheel will not do.

Carbon paper

This is for transferring double-thickness markings.

Pencils

Hard pencils (H or 2H). Coloured fibre-tip pens are also useful.

Long ruler or straight edge

Tape measure

This should be marked in centimetres. If you have not yet tried working in centimetres, now is the time to do so. The metric system is actually much easier to use than the imperial system, and you should not attempt to convert one to the other; this is why alternative inch measurements are not given. Just take the centimetres as they come – one soon gets over the shock of one's hip measurement hovering around the hundred mark.

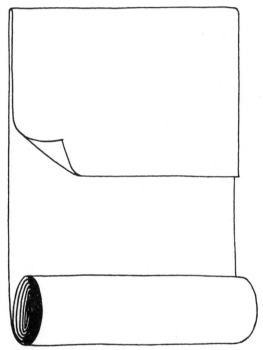

Figure 1

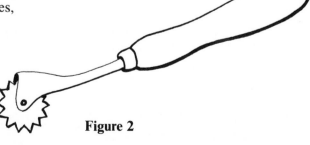

Figure 2

PERSONAL MEASUREMENT CHART

Ten body measurements are needed for constructing the blouse pattern blocks. You must have the help of a friend to measure you; it is impossible to do this accurately for yourself.

Measurements should be taken closely but not tightly. The extra ease needed for arm movement in the blouse should not be allowed for as it is built into the block patterns (*Figure 3*).

1 Bust, taken over the fullest part. (At the back the tape measure should be kept high across the shoulder blades)_____cm
Quarter bust measurement_____cm
One twelfth bust measurement_____cm

2 Waist_____cm

3 Hip, taken over the widest part of the hip usually 20–22 cm below the waist_____cm
Quarter hip measurement_____cm

4 Back width, taken 10 cm below the prominent bone at the nape of the neck, from one armhole seam to the other. If in doubt, be generous here_____cm
Half back width_____cm

5 Back waist length, taken from the prominent bone at the nape down to the waistline. (Tie a piece of string round the waist to show its true level)_____cm
Half back waist length_____cm
Quarter back waist length_____cm

6 Bust point width – the measurement between the points of the bust_____cm
Half bust point width_____cm

7 Shoulder to bust point length, taken from the centre of the shoulder seam down to the point of the bust_____cm

8 Arm length, taken from the shoulder bone to the wrist bone, round the elbow, with the arm slightly bent. Be generous here_____cm

9 Arm girth, taken round the fullest part of the upper arm_____cm

10 Wrist girth, taken loosely just above the wrist bone_____cm

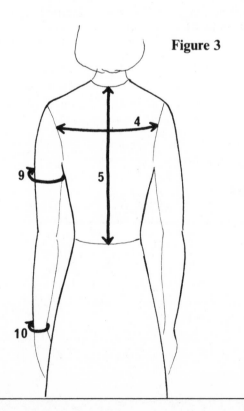

Figure 3

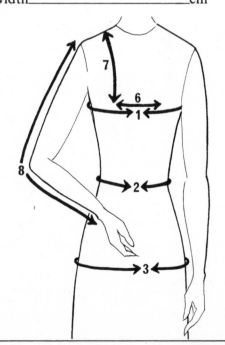

DRAFTING THE BLOCKS

Block patterns are not fashion shapes and contain no styling. Nor do they include seam and hem allowances; so they cannot be used directly as dressmaking patterns. They are simply the essential record of your bone structure, from which the final pattern is built. Even changes in your weight will not substantially affect the fit. A couple of centimetres more, or less, on hip or bust or waist just means that you need to add or subtract a quarter of that amount on the side seam edges of the final pattern – which you can do without cutting a new block. The blocks provide, however, a permanent fit for the important measurements across the back, and down the back from neck to waist, on which the proportions of the pattern depend.

DRAWING CURVES

Pattern drafting consists mainly of measuring and ruling straight lines, but sometimes you will need to draw curved lines joining three or more points. Here is the simplest way to draw a smooth curve.

Always draw from the inside of the curve, so that the movement of your hand goes naturally with the line rather than against it. If you draw as shown in *Figure 4*, you will have less control over your pencil, and the line may wobble. But turn the paper round, draw as shown in *Figure 5* and the movement of your hand will then assist the curve.

For a full curve, rest the heel of your hand on the paper and use it as a pivot. For a very shallow curve, use your elbow as a pivot. Draw quickly: the curve will be smoother than if you tense your fingers and go slowly.

FOLDING IN DARTS

It is easy to draw in the two sides of a dart; less easy to shape the seamline from which the dart springs. The following method is foolproof and should be used for darts in any part of a garment.

1 Draw in the provisional seamline as a straight line, A–B (*Figure 6*). Mark in the two sides of the dart, C–D and E–D.

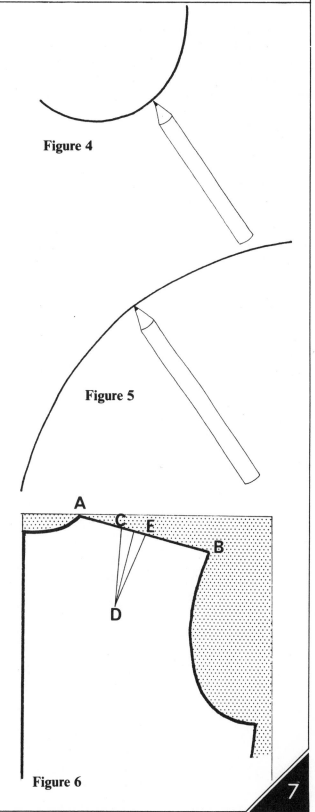

Figure 4

Figure 5

Figure 6

2 Lay the paper across the corner of a table, with the lower part of the pattern hanging over the edge. With the point of the dart – D – on the corner of the table, crease the pattern from C to D and bring the crease over to the line E–D, matching the sides of the dart accurately (*Figure 7*).

3 This folding will bend the seamline; so, still with the dart folded, rule a new straight line between A and B. Cut along this line and unfold the dart. *Figure 8* shows the shape of the final seamline.

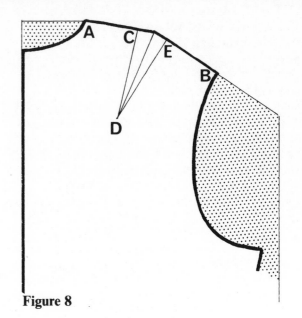

Figure 8

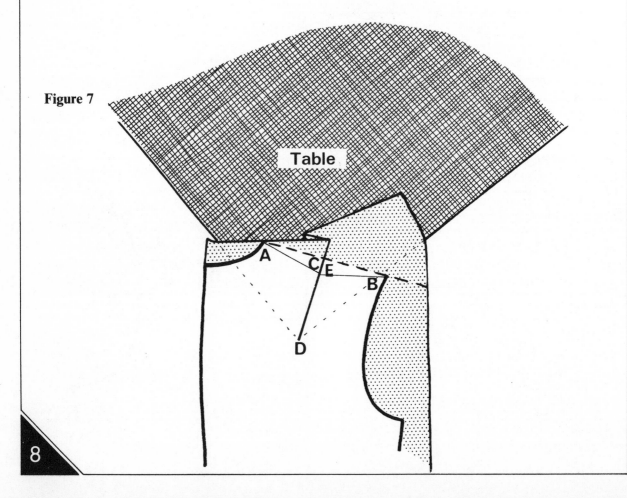

Figure 7

DRAFTING THE BACK BLOCK
Cut a rectangle of lining paper:

Length – your back waist length plus 22 cm;
Width – quarter hip plus 2 cm.

Make sure, as shown in *Figure 1*, that the top and bottom edges are at right angles to the sides.
Mark A at the top left-hand corner (*Figure 9*).
Measuring down the left-hand edge:

A–B is 1·5 cm;
B–C is 2·5 cm;
B–D is a quarter of the back waist length;
B–E is half the back waist length plus 2 cm;
B–F is back waist length;
Mark G at the bottom left-hand corner.

Crease right across the paper from C, D, E and F, parallel to the top edge as shown in *Figure 9*.

Measuring across:

A–H is one twelfth of bust, minus 0·5 cm;
C–J is half back width, plus 1·5 cm;
D–K is half back width, plus 0·5 cm;
Mark L at the mid-point of D–K;
E–M is the same length as D–K;
E–N is a quarter of bust, plus 1·5 cm;
F–P is a quarter of bust, minus 0·5 cm;
G–Q is the same length as D–L;
Mark R at the bottom right-hand corner.

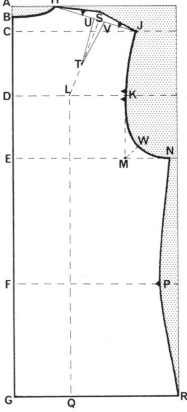

Figure 9

For the neckline
Join B–H with a shallow curve. This line is horizontal for the first 2 cm.

For the shoulderline and darts
Join H–J for the provisional shoulderline.
H–S is 7 cm.
Join S–L; T is 7·5 cm from S down this line.
U and V are 0·5 cm to each side of S.
Join U–T–V for the shoulder dart.
Now fold in the dart, as in *Figures 6, 7 and 8*.
Rule a line from H to J, across the fold, cut along the line and unfold the dart. This gives the final shoulderline.
Join L–Q. This line gives the position of any back waist dart you may wish to add later.

For the armhole
Join K–M.
Draw a diagonal line 2·5 cm long, from M to W.

Join J–K–W–N in a smooth curve. (J–K is slightly hollowed; K–W–N is a fuller curve.)

For the side seam
Join N–P–R, curving round at P.

Balance marks
Mark a notch at P and at each side of the shoulder dart. Mark a double notch at K.

Cut out the block
Discard the shaded areas shown on *Figure 9*.

DRAFTING THE FRONT BLOCK

Cut a rectangle of paper the same length but 5 cm wider than the one used for the back block (*Figure 10*).
Place the back block on the paper, matching the lower and left-hand edges, with H (the neck point of the shoulderline) touching the top edge.

As shown by the thin line, draw all round the back block, except for the shoulderline H–J. Join H–J with a straight line for the moment.

Draw in the lines D–K, E–N and F–P.
Mark in the points G and R.
Remove the back block.

For the side seam
Draw in the seamline 1 cm to the right of the line N–P–R; mark in A, B and C as shown.

For the neckline
Mark L at the top left-hand corner of the paper.
L–M down the left-hand edge is 1·5 cm more than the neck width L–H. Join M–H for the front neckline: this is almost a quarter circle.

For the waist dart
D–Q is half the bust point width;
G–S is half the bust point width.
Join Q–S to give the position of any front waist dart you may wish to add later.

For the shoulder shaping
Extend the line H–J to the edge of the paper.
Measuring along this line:
H–T is 6·5 cm;
T–U (the width of the bust dart) is the same as the front neck width L–H;
J–V (along the extended line) is 1 cm *less* than the length T–U.
Measure 1 cm down from V and mark W.

For the bust dart
Measure the shoulder to bust point length from T down to X, letting X fall on the line running down from Q–S. This gives one side of the dart. Join U–X for the other side.

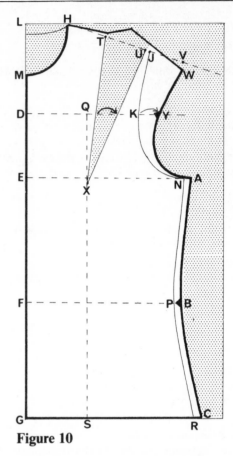

Figure 10

Fold in the dart as in *Figures 6*, *7* and *8*, redraw the shoulder as a straight line from H to W, cut along this line and unfold the dart. (Check that the back and front shoulders, less their darts, are the same length.)

For the armhole
Measure the width of the dart at the level of the line D–K (shown by the arrow on *Figure 10*).
Extend D–K to the right by the same measurement as the dart width and mark Y.
Join W–Y–A for the front armhole. (W–Y is slightly hollowed; Y–A is a full curve.)

Balance marks
Mark notches at Y and B.

Cut out the block
Discard the shaded areas.

DRAFTING THE BLOCKS

DRAFTING THE SLEEVE BLOCK

Cut a rectangle of paper:
Length – arm length plus 2 cm;
Width – arm girth plus 8 cm;

Figure 11. Crease down the centre of the paper and mark A at the top of the crease.

Crease sides-to-middle, so that the edges meet on the first crease, from A downwards. Open out the paper.

On the back and front blocks, measure the armhole curves J–N (*Figure 9*) and W–A (*Figure 10*). This is easiest if you measure with the tape on its edge, so that it can follow the curve (*Figure 12*). Add these two measurements together to obtain the armhole girth. Divide armhole girth by three.

This length (about 14–15 cm) will be the sleevehead depth. Measure this length down the left-hand edge of the paper and mark B. Crease across the paper to C.

Join B–A–C.

Mark D and E where these lines cross the creases.

To shape the sleevehead

Measure to the midpoint of B–D, then measure 0·5 cm inside the line and mark F.

Measure 1 cm outside the line at D and mark G.

Measure to the midpoint of D–A, then measure 2 cm outside the line and mark H.

Measure to the midpoint of A–E, then measure 2·5 cm outside the line and mark J.

Measure 1 cm outside the line at E and mark K.

Measure to the midpoint of E–C, then measure 1·5 cm inside the line and mark L.

Draw in the sleevehead through the points B–F–G–H–A–J–K–L–C. (The curve is shallower at the back of the sleevehead between B and A; more pronounced at the front of the sleevehead between A and C.)

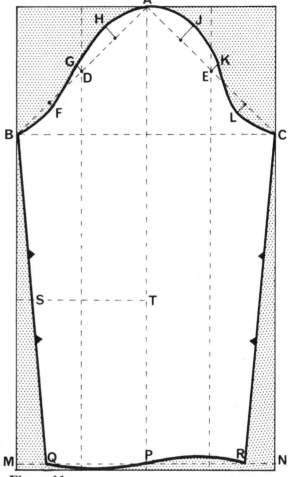

Figure 11

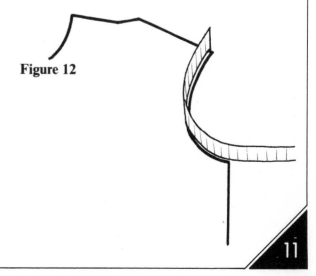

Figure 12

To shape the sleeve

Measure 1 cm up from the bottom corners of the paper and mark M and N.

Join M–N and mark P at the centre.

Measure 4 cm to the right of M and mark Q.

Measure 4 cm to the left of N and mark R.

Join B–Q for the back edge of the sleeve, and C–R for the front edge.

To shape the wrist edge

Draw a curve from Q to R for the wristline, dropping 1 cm (to the bottom of the paper) between Q and P, and rising 1 cm between P and R.

For the elbowline

Mark S at the midpoint of B–Q. Crease across from S to T. This is the position for any elbow dart you may wish to make later on. Mark notches above and below S; fold the sleeve in half down the centre line, and mark corresponding notches on the other edge.

Cut out, discarding the shaded areas.

CHECKING THE CURVES

The back and front

1 Place the back and front blocks together along the shoulder seam, matching at their neck ends. There should be an unbroken curve round the neckline. Re-cut (only a millimetre or two) if needed to smooth out the curve. Mark a notch on the front shoulder to match the back notch (*Figure 13*).

2 Now match the shoulderlines at their armhole ends, check and if necessary re-cut to smooth out the curve there. Mark a notch on the front shoulder to match the second notch on the back (*Figure 14*).

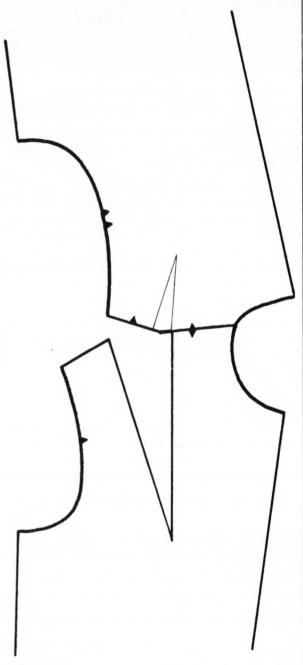

Figure 13

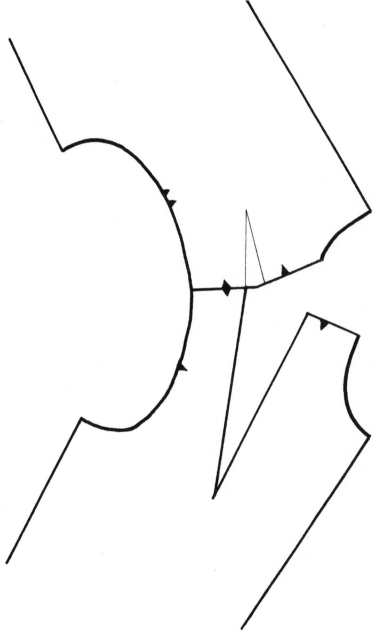

Figure 14

3 Match the sides of the blocks, from the armhole downwards; check for a smooth curve under the armhole (*Figure 15*).

The sleeve
1 Fold the sleeve block edges-to-middle, matching B to C and Q to R. Check the smoothness of the curves at armhole and wrist (*Figure 16*).

2 Now place the sleeve and back blocks *right sides together*, matching the underarm points. Following the curves, swing the sleevehead round the lower part of the bodice armhole until K is reached (*Figure 17*). Mark a pair of corresponding notches on the sleevehead. (The double notch will distinguish the back edge of the sleeve and make it impossible to sew the wrong sleeve into the wrong armhole – otherwise an easy trap for the unwary.)

3 Repeat with the front block and the front edge of the sleevehead placed as in *Figure 18* and mark a notch level with Y.

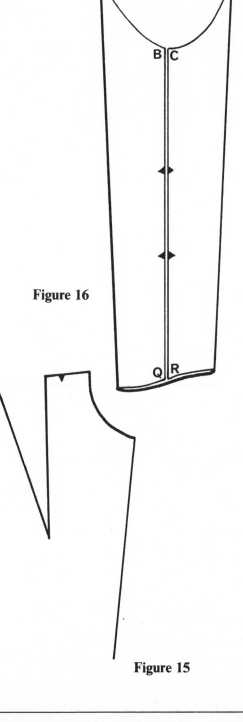

Figure 16

Figure 15

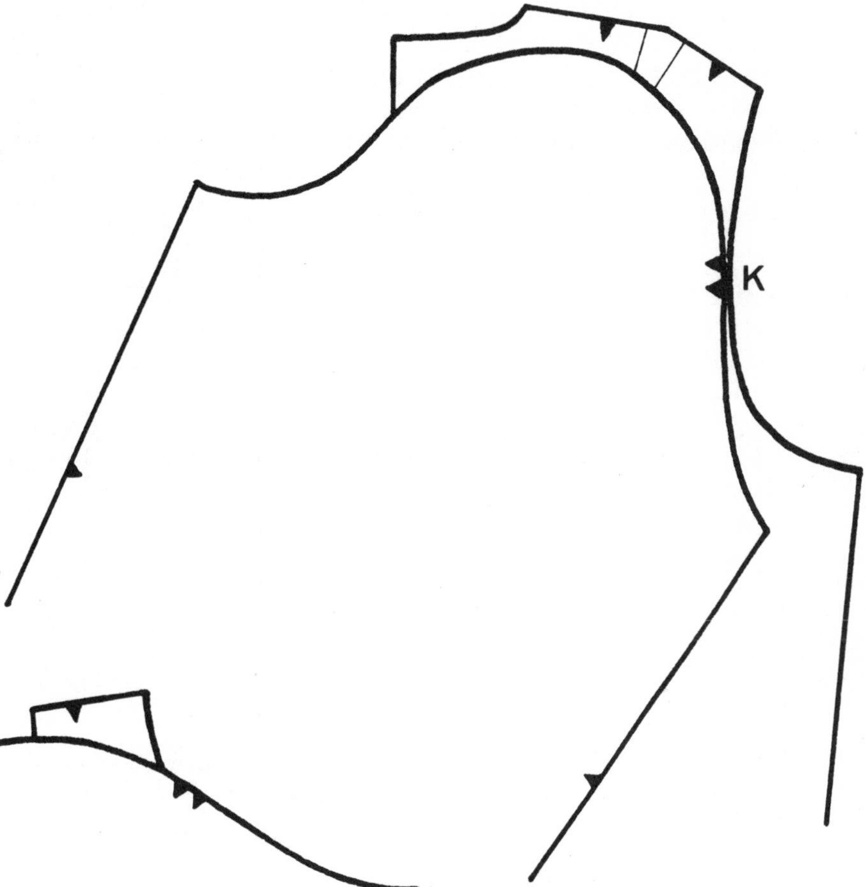

Figure 17

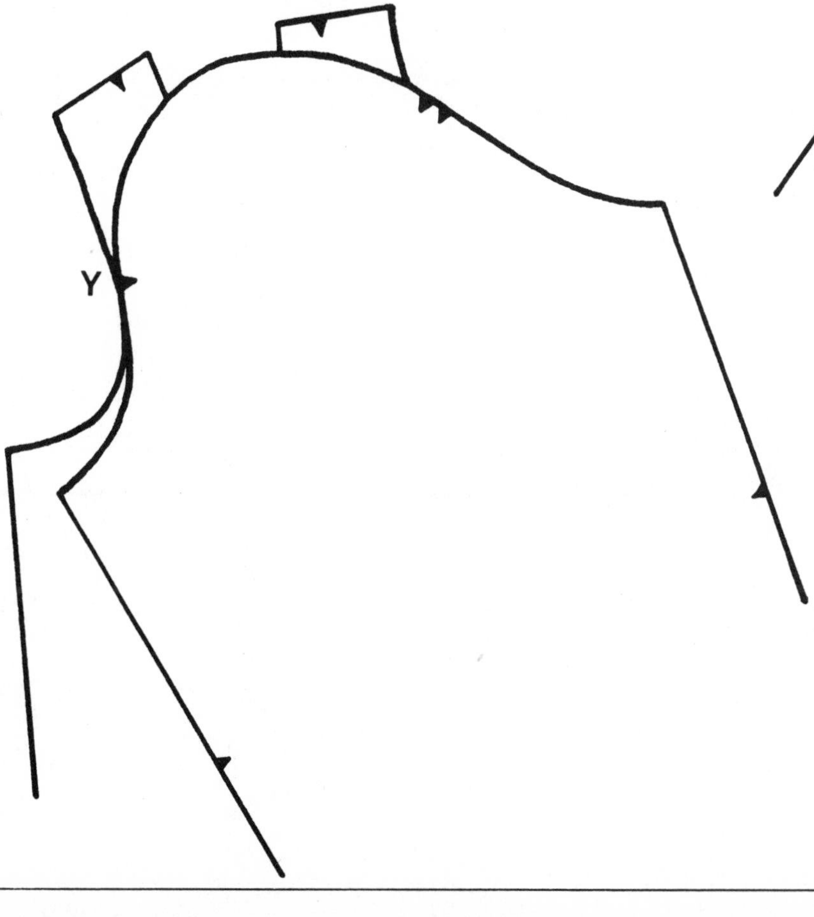

K

Figure 18

Y

DRAFTING THE BLOCKS

TRANSFERRING THE BLOCKS TO CARD

Now that the block patterns have been drafted, you should transfer their outlines on to sheets of thin card.

The back
Place the back block over a sheet of card and draw accurately round its outline (*Figure 19*). With the tracing wheel mark in with perforations:

the dart;
the line L–Q (the line for a waist dart which also serves as the straight-grain line);
the line F–P (waist level).
Cut out the block, cut the notches inwards and label the block with its name.

The front
Place the front block over a sheet of card and draw round its edges. With the tracing wheel, mark in *heavily* so that the marks will show on the reverse of the card:

the line X–S (the line for a waist dart, which also serves as a straight-grain line);
the line F–B (the waist level).

Cut out the card block, turn it over and mark its name (*Figure 20*). From now on, that side of the block is used as the right side – in both senses. It now relates to the right-hand side of the body and corresponds to the back block – which also relates to the right-hand side of the body.

The sleeve
Draw round the outline over card (*Figure 21*). Mark in:

the line A–P as a straight-grain line;
the elbow dart line S–T and the back arm line below it;
the line B–C.

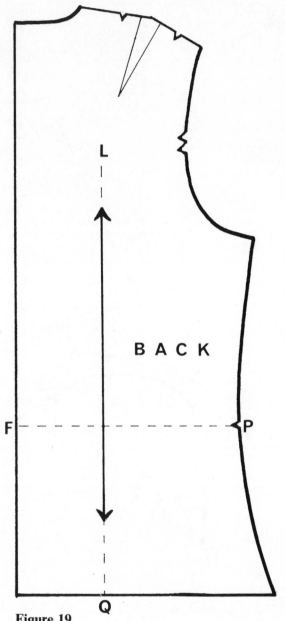

Figure 19

DRAFTING THE BLOCKS

As the sleeve is already drafted for the right arm, your blocks form a complete record for that side of the body.

The blocks are now ready to be used for developing whatever style of blouse you may want. They themselves are not working patterns, but templets; they are never cut or altered in any way. The final pattern, with all the design details as well as the seam and hem allowances, will be traced from them.

The blocks should last indefinitely. Drafting them is a once-for-all operation. To store them, punch a hole near the top of each block, thread a piece of tape through the holes and hang them from a coathanger. As your collection of blocks for different types of garments grows, the coathangers can be hung flat at the back of a wardrobe where they will take up no space.

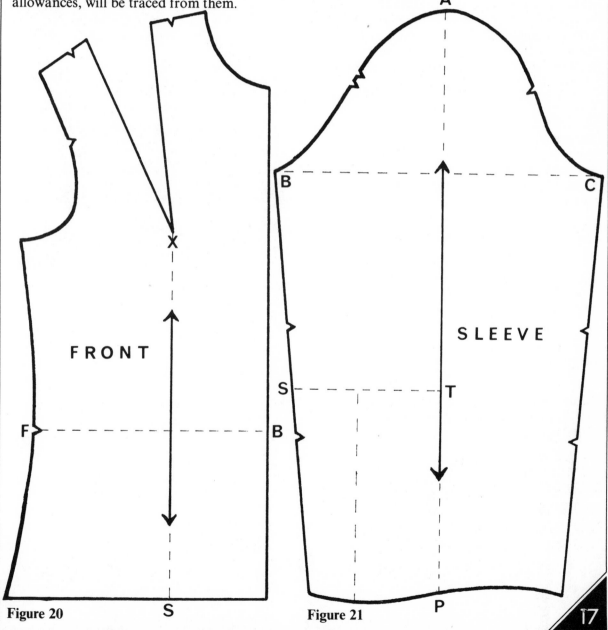

Figure 20

Figure 21

The next step is to consider the style of blouse or shirt you are ready to develop from the blocks.

Do you want a front-buttoned opening or a back zip; a high or low neckline, with what kind of collar; loose, puffed or fitting sleeves? The combinations are endless. It is important to think of the design as a whole, with a relationship in style between the various features. Cuffs and collar, for instance, should be similar in shape; the same top-stitching detail could appear on collar and pocket; gathers into a yoke could be repeated in sleeve gathers, or a front yoke repeated at the back.

This section gives instructions for cutting a wide variety of styles. Rather than read the whole section, it is suggested that you browse through the diagrams for ideas. *Figure 22* shows a group of body outlines. On thin paper placed over these you could trace and sketch out the effect of different necklines, collars or sleeves until you have evolved a complete design. Then just pick out the instructions for the particular details you need and disregard the rest.

Take plenty of time deciding: it is quite easy at this stage to work out a pattern for any design – much more difficult, and possibly wasteful in material, to change your ideas later on.

THE DRAFT PATTERN
You do not use the blocks directly as patterns. You simply draw round their outlines on fresh pieces of paper and on those add any styling you want. This often means cutting the draft pattern (not the block) into pieces to add the fullnesss of pleats or gathers. In that case, the final outline is drawn round the cut pieces on yet another sheet of paper. Lastly, seam and hem allowances are added and the final pattern cut out. An example of the whole process is shown in the illustration on page 45.

Square-necked blouse with gathers set into the yoke

Figure 22

DESIGNING THE PATTERN

The sequence of designing the different parts of the shirt or blouse should be:

1 The body shaping – darts, pleats, gathers or tucks; and the yokes that may go with them.

2 The position of the opening – back-neckline or front-buttoned; and the facings needed for the opening.

3 The collar, if any.

4 The sleeves and cuffs.

5 The pockets.

6 The length – to the waist or hip.

The instructions that follow are therefore given in this order.

THE BODY SHAPING

Darts

In the block the bust dart (which shapes the front) is drawn from the shoulder seam. This is the most convenient position for it in plainly-cut blouse fronts, such as those in *Figure 23*, and for front-opening shirt styles. For any of these, just draw round the block without making any alterations.

However, the dart can if you wish be moved to the side seam. This will make a simpler pattern for styles with yokes (*Figure 24*).

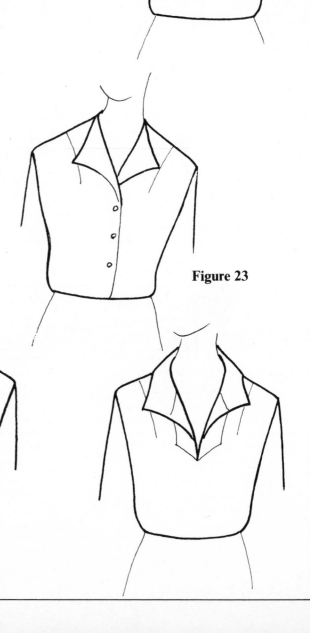

Figure 23

20

Figure 24

DESIGNING THE PATTERN

1 Trace the front block outline on to paper and cut it out.

2 Cut from the side seam to the point of the dart (*Figure 25*).

3 Move the armhole part of the pattern round to close the shoulder dart – this will open a side dart.

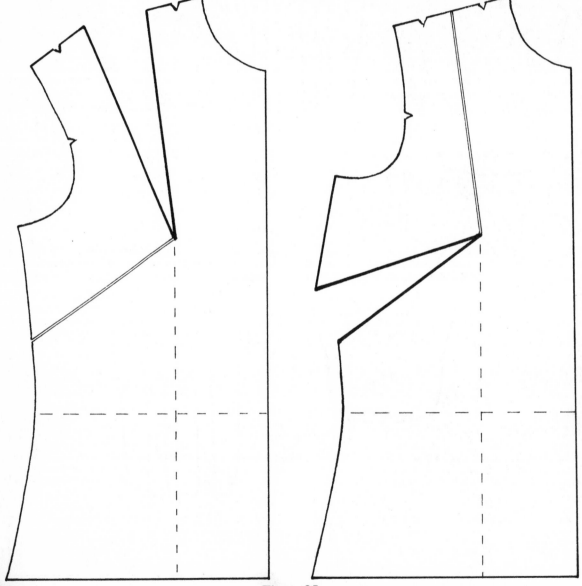

Figure 25

4 Draw the new outline on fresh paper.

The dart is drawn to the point of the bust in order that it can be pivoted round into another seam if necessary. It is *not* stitched to that length, but shortened 3 cm to leave more fabric at the point and give a softer shape. For the final fitting line, redraw the dart as shown in *Figure 26*.

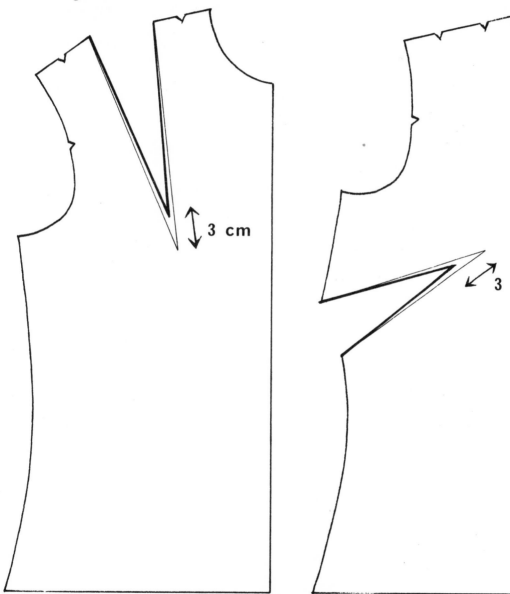

Figure 26

Fullness from a yoke

The yoke can be a setting for pleats, tucks or gathers as in the photograph on page 18. Whatever the shape you choose for the yoke, the draft pattern is made in the same way.

1 Begin by moving the dart to the side seam, as described on page 22.

2 Draw in the line for the yoke, mark notches near each end of the line and cut off the yoke piece (*Figure 27*).

3 Add whatever extra width you need below the yoke by cutting down the pattern through the point of the dart and spreading the pieces apart. The cut edges are kept parallel and the waistlines level (*Figure 28*).

4 The distance you spread the pieces apart depends on the amount of fullness you intend to add, and on whether you plan for gathers, tucks or pleats – as in the following instructions.

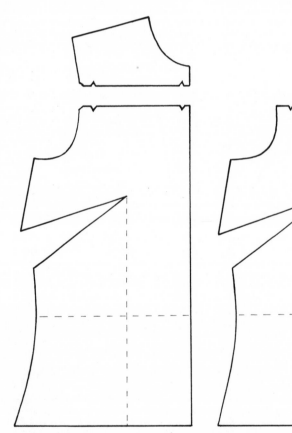

Figure 27   **Figure 28**

Gathers

For slightly gathered styles add 2–5 cm; for a fully-gathered design add 5–10 cm. *Figure 29* shows the way you would add gathers to a curved yoke (such as the top left-hand sketch in *Figure 24*) and how you would redraw the gathering line between the notches.

Tucks

Work out the extra amount of fullness needed for the tucks. Pin-tucks each take up 0·5 cm extra width, so four pin-tucks, as shown in the top right-hand sketch of *Figure 24*, would mean the addition of only 2 cm extra width to the pattern.

Blind-tucks (those touching each other, as shown in the centre-top sketch) need the addition of *twice* their own width. Therefore three tucks each 1 cm wide would need an extra 6 cm. Draw round the altered outline on fresh paper. Mark in the crease-line of each tuck, and its two stitching lines which will be matched together (*Figure 30*).

Pleats

Pleats are added to the pattern in the same way as tucks but are not stitched down over the bust. (See *Figure 74*)

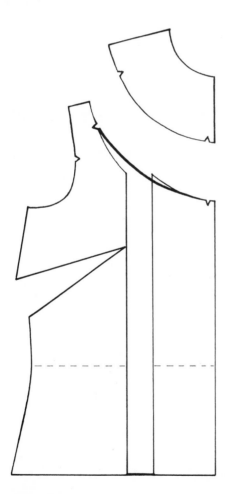

Figure 29

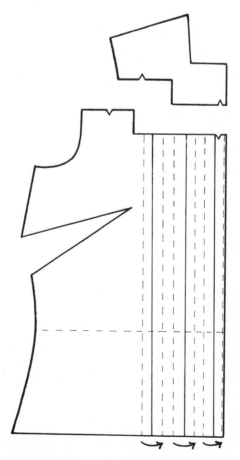

Figure 30

However, you should mark their lines right down the pattern as a guide to pressing them into place. You may later wish to stitch them for a short distance at waist level.

Each pleat needs the addition of double its own width to the pattern. *Figure 31* shows how to add pleats below a sloping yoke, such as the one in the bottom-right sketch of *Figure 24*. Pleat the paper first, then trace and cut the seamline, and unfold.

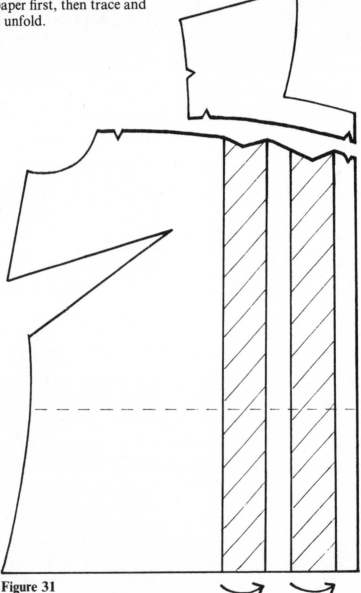

Figure 31

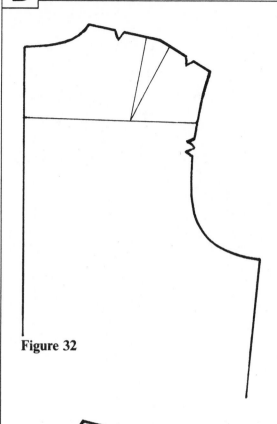

Figure 32

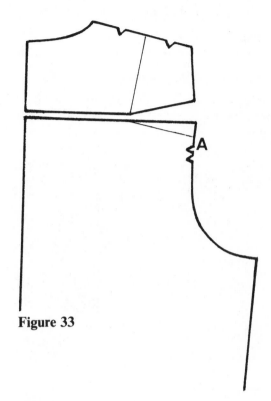

Figure 33

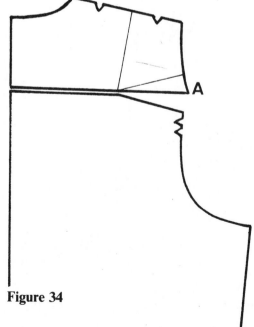

Figure 34

Back yokes

A back yoke, like a front one, can be cut to any shape you choose and can in the same way form a setting for gathers or pleats.

The yoke should replace the back shoulder dart.

1 Draw round the back block outline and cut out.

2 Draw and cut along the yoke line (*Figure 32*).

3 Close the shoulder dart (*Figure 33*). Mark A at the armhole, 1 cm below the yoke line. Trim off a wedge 7·5 cm long, from A towards the centre-back.

4 Transfer this wedge to the yoke (*Figure 34*). The sloping line now left at the armhole will exactly replace the dart shaping, while retaining a straight lower edge to the yoke.

NECKLINES, OPENINGS AND FACINGS

Necklines

The block gives a round, fitted neckline which would need an opening – either at the back or, with buttoning, down the front. But if you choose a lower cut neckline, you may not need an opening at all. A low scoop or V-neck could be made deep enough to slip over your head – see *Figure 35* and the blouse below.

Scoop-necked blouse with flounced collar and contrast binding

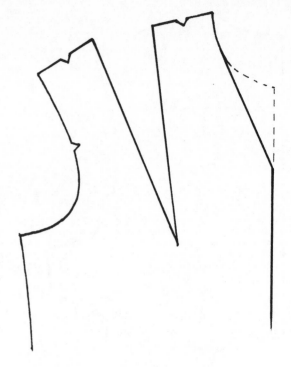

Figure 35

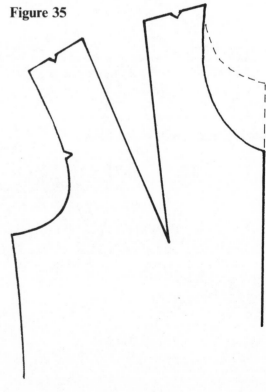

DESIGNING THE PATTERN

For any shape of neckline you will need to cut back and front neck facings, both to finish the edge and as a setting for any collar. Trace round the necklines of back and front blocks; the facings should not be less than 5 cm wide (*Figure 36*).

Another choice could be a neckline gathered with a drawstring or elastic (*Figure 37*). The pattern alteration looks formidable but is actually quite simple.

Figure 37

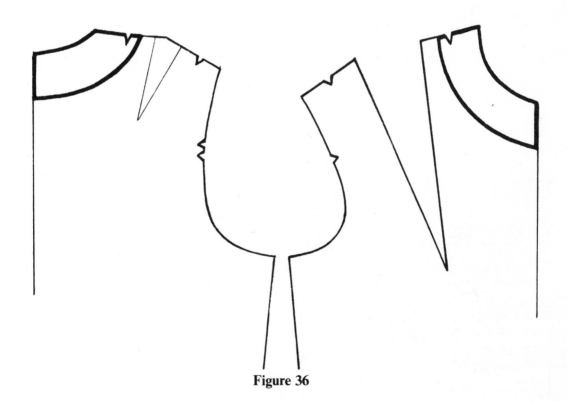

Figure 36

DESIGNING THE PATTERN

1 Transfer the front dart to the side seam (*Figure 25*). The back dart is not affected.

2 Trim the neckline to the desired depth.

3 Cut the front and back patterns from the neckline to within a couple of millimetres of the side seam, as shown in *Figure 38*.

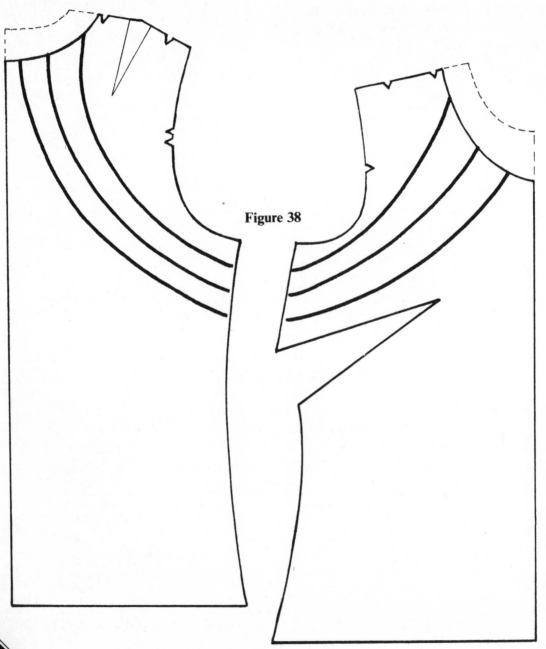

Figure 38

4 Spread apart along the neckline (*Figure 39*). The new neckline should measure not less than 60 cm; so in the drafted half-patterns the back and front should total at least 30 cm.

5 Draw in the new outlines as shown. As these edges would be finished with a narrow casing of bias binding, no facings are needed.

Back opening

No pattern alteration is made for a short back opening, finished with either a zip or a hook and eye. Facings should be cut as in *Figure 36*.

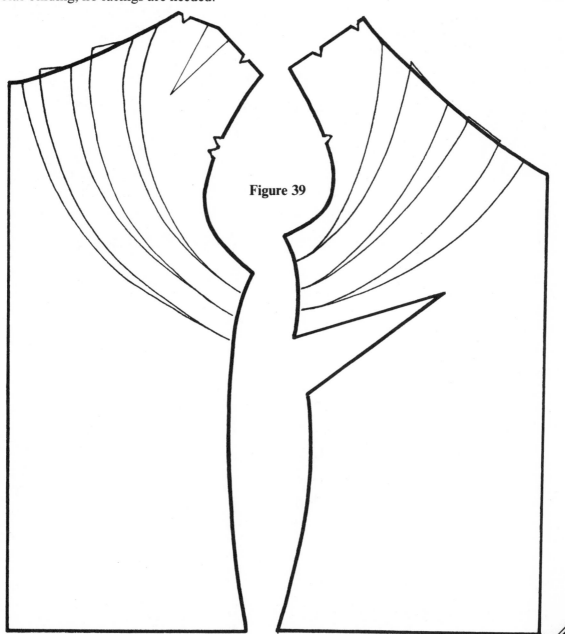

Figure 39

DESIGNING THE PATTERN

Front faced opening

Openings such as those shown in *Figure 40* can be finished with bias binding if the style calls for it; but facings will give a crisper, cleaner edge. The photograph on page 48 shows such an opening, used where the blouse is gathered into a neckband.

Front buttoned opening

For a shirt-front design, the extension for buttons and buttonholes is added to the centre-front of the pattern. A full-length facing is cut in one piece with the front.

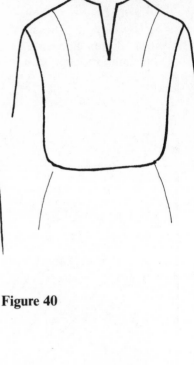

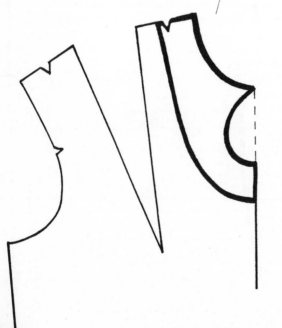

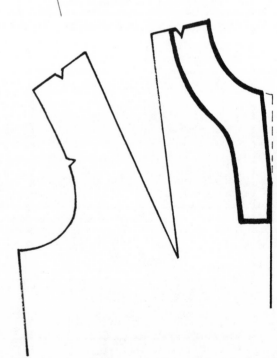

Figure 40

DESIGNING THE PATTERN

1 Make a crease A–B, 20 cm from the right-hand edge of a piece of pattern paper. Fold that edge under, along the crease (*Figure 41*).

2 Rule a line C–D, 2 cm to the left of the fold.

3 Place the draft pattern for the front over the paper, matching its centre-front to the ruled line C–D (*Figure 42*).

4 Draw round the outline and cut out. At the centre-front, cut straight out to the fold as shown by the arrows.

Figure 41

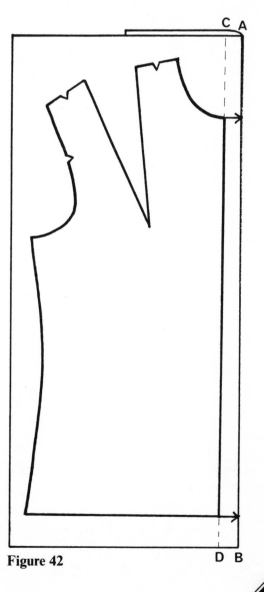

Figure 42

5 Open out the pattern. Draw in and cut along the free edge of the facing. At the shoulder, the facing should be the same width as the back facing – not less than 5 cm (*Figure 43*).

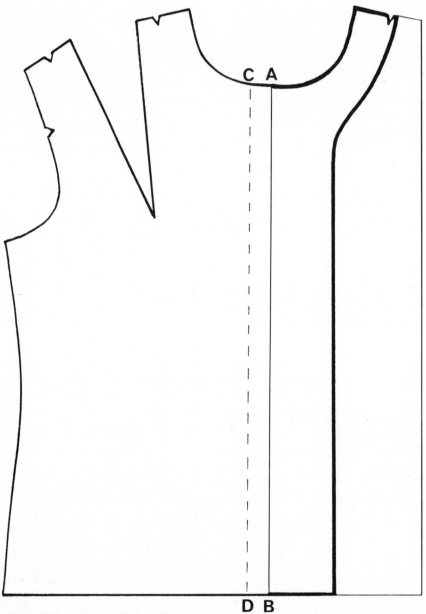

Figure 43

Front-buttoned opening with separate facing
It is not always possible to cut the facing in
one with the blouse front. Revers shaped
outwards below a wide collar, as in *Figure 44*,
will need a separately cut facing. Draw round
the front block outline, add a 2 cm button-
stand extension and shape out the revers as
desired (up to about 5 cm), from the level of
the dart point upwards. Draw in free edge of
the facing.

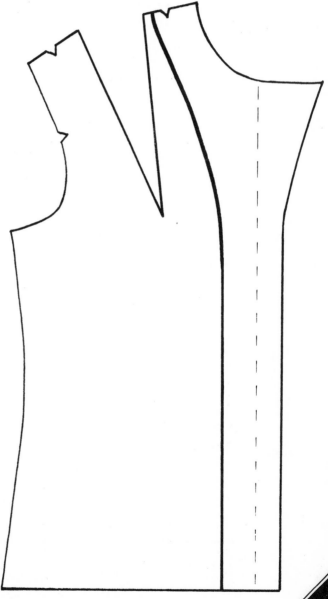

Figure 44

DESIGNING THE PATTERN

Figure 45 shows another blouse shape that would need separate facings.

COLLARS

The length of a collar is simple to determine: it is as long as the blouse neckline. That is the *only* simple fact about collars. Beyond that, they can be infinitely varied in their height at the back of the neck, their breadth and their style. A collar is not unduly difficult to draft; the difficulty lies in visualizing its finished appearance before you have made it up.

It is no bad plan to cut your chosen collar shape from a scrap of any similar fabric, tack it round the neckline of the partly-made blouse and see how it looks on you. This test will also give you a much clearer idea of the width you want and the style line of the outer edge.

Figure 45

In general, collars shaped like the letter C will lie flat at the neck and on the shoulders, Peter Pan style. Straight-cut collars, like the letter I, will stand high round the neck. A collar with some stand at the back is usually a more becoming frame for the face, so a straighter shape is generally preferable to a very curved one.

Shirt collars with a high stand
These can be quite straight, or only very slightly shaped, along the neckline. The stand at the back will be half the total depth of the collar (*Figure 46*).

1 Measure the neckline of the back and of the front pattern, with the tape measure on edge as in *Figure 12*. This combined length gives you the collar neck measurement, from centre-back to centre-front (not including any overlap for buttoning).

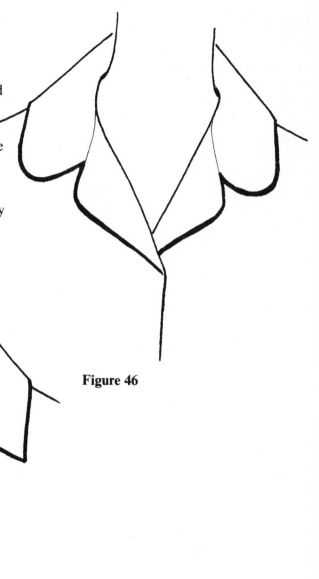

Figure 46

2 *Figure 47*. The neck edge of the collar is A–B, a straight line. A–C is the back neck measurement and C–B the front neck. Mark a notch at C.

3 A–D, at right angles to A–B, is the depth of the collar at the centre-back, including the stand. 10 cm is a generous measurement – much less than this can look skimped.

4 D–E is three-quarters of the length of A–B, and parallel to it.

5 Between B and E, draw in any style line you choose for a pointed or rounded collar. (With a high stand you cannot widen the collar any further back than E as it would not lie properly over the shoulder.)

6 If you want a slightly closer fit at the front of the collar, trim off a narrow wedge from F to G. (F is 6 cm from B; G is 0·5 cm below B.)

7 The centre-back, A–D, is placed to a fold of the fabric, so mark in a fold-arrow.

8 For a collar that buttons through the stand, the front edge should be cut to the length of the neckline *plus* overlap. The stand is then curved back to the centre-front line, and the fall of the collar drawn from there (see the blouse on page 46).

Collars with a low stand

Flat collars – such as the Peter Pan, Puritan and Byronic shapes in *Figure 48* – can be drawn directly on the back and front blouse patterns. This has the advantage of showing the proportion of the collar against the bodice.

1 Lay the back and front patterns on drafting paper, with the shoulder lines together. Match the neck points exactly, but overlap the patterns 0·5 cm at the darts (*Figure 49*).

2 Draw on the patterns the style lines for the outer and front edges of the collar (*Figure 50*). The line should join the centre-back of the bodice at a right angle.

3 With the tracing wheel, mark these lines and the neckline. Mark a notch to show the position of the shoulder seam. *Figure 51* shows the other two collar shapes.

4 This minimum amount of overlap at the shoulder line will give you a very flat collar, which will stand up only enough to hide the neckline seam; but it can be as wide as you like over the shoulder. For a collar with a higher stand, overlap the back and front patterns a little further – to 1 cm or even 1·5 cm at the dart – still keeping the neck points matched. The overlap has the effect of shortening and therefore pulling up the outer edge of the collar; so the final pattern will be less curved.

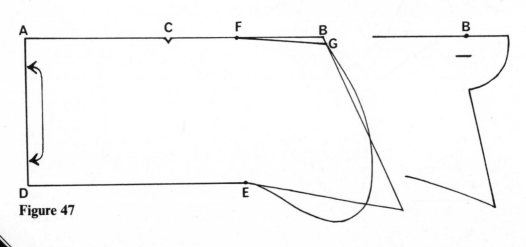

Figure 47

Figure 48

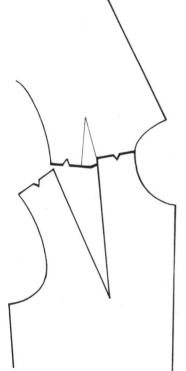

Figure 49

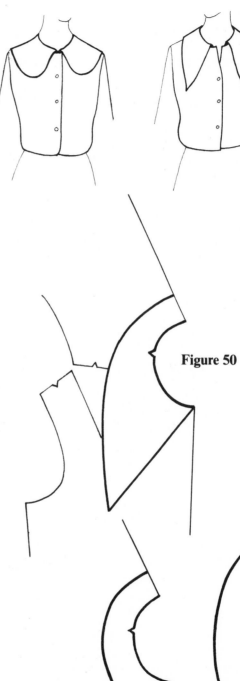

Figure 50

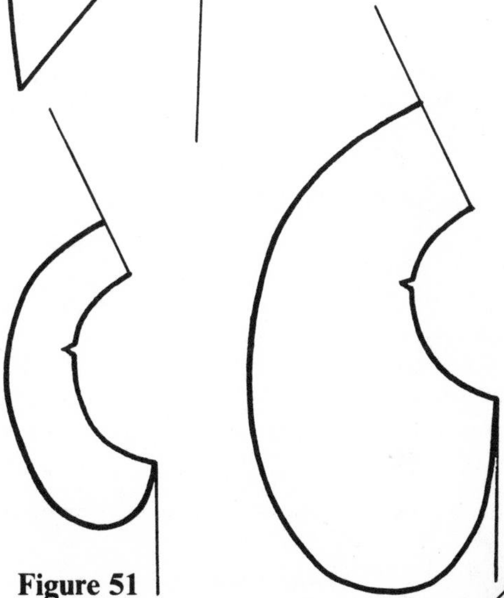

Figure 51

Mandarin collars

A very simple collar to draft and make
(*Figure 52*). To prevent its poking forward,
the upper edge is slightly tightened.

1 Draw a rectangle the length of the blouse
neckline. (You are drafting the whole collar,
not a half-pattern.) The height of the
rectangle should be the height of the collar –
between 3 and 5 cm (*Figure 53*).

2 Mark notches where the collar is to match
the shoulder seams. Make four cuts from the
upper almost to the lower edge of the pattern.

3 Overlap the pieces 0·5 cm at the top of each
cut. Curve off the front corners as shown, and
draw the new outline. Mark in a straight-
grain arrow.

Tie collars

A tie collar is cut as a straight strip (*Figure
54*). No neck shaping is needed if it is cut on
the true cross. The tie should be seamed along
one edge only, so cut the pattern twice as wide
as the finished tie ends – about 12 cm, folding

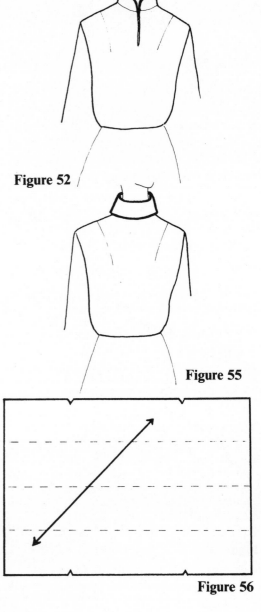

Figure 52

Figure 55

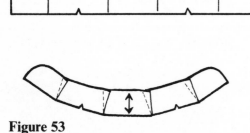

Figure 53

Figure 56

Figure 54

to 6 cm. The length should be 1·80–2 metres; to obtain this length you will therefore need at least one seam, parallel to the straight grain and diagonally across the tie.

Polo collars

This type of collar (*Figure 55*) sits best if cut on the true cross of the fabric. As it is in double thickness, and then folded down, it must be cut four times its finished depth. The length is the same as the blouse neckline from centre-back to centre-back. *Figure 56* Mark in the shoulder seam positions with notches, and mark a straight-grain arrow on the exact diagonal.

Flounced collars

The shape of the graceful collar shown in the photograph on page 28 is achieved by making the free, outer edge longer than the neck edge. Such collars drape more gently if they are made up in single thickness and finished with a very narrow hem or with binding.

1 Match the back and front bodice patterns at the shoulder seam. Do not overlap.

2 Draw in the lines of the collar; the flounce will hang best if it is cut rather deeper in front (*Figure 57*). Cut out the collar.

3 Divide the collar into 12 sections. Cut from the outer edge to within 0·2 cm of the neckline (*Figure 58*).

4 For a very full flounce such as this, you will need to make the collar in three sections seamed together. So cut right through between numbers 4 and 5 marked on the diagram.

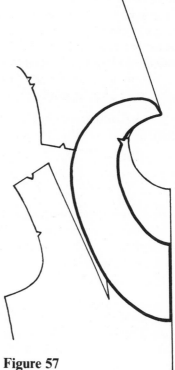

Figure 57

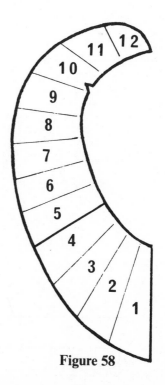

Figure 58

5 Now spread numbers 1–4 into a half-circle as shown in *Figure 59*. (Number 1 will be placed to a fold, and number 4 should end up on the straight grain, parallel to the fold.) Spread numbers 5–12 into a full circle; this section will be cut from double fabric with the edge of number 5 on the straight grain.

6 Draw in the new outlines to link the pieces. You will have to leave room for seam allowances, so these have been drawn in as dotted lines.

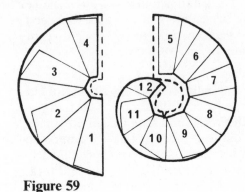

Figure 59

SLEEVES

The block sleeve is wide enough to give a little fullness at the cuff. The shirts shown in the photographs on pages 44 and 46 both have sleeves cut to the block width. It is a good general-purpose shape for most designs, without any alteration.

Short sleeves

The lower edge of a short sleeve is not straight, but curved to give a better line round the arm.

1 Trace round the block and cut out the pattern to the length you want (*Figure 60*).

2 Fold the pattern edges-to-middle, with the side edges exactly matched (*Figure 61*). The corners will be higher than the centre of the sleeve. Rule a line straight across, cut along the line and unfold (*Figure 62*).

3 The final shape will be smoothly curved at the hem.

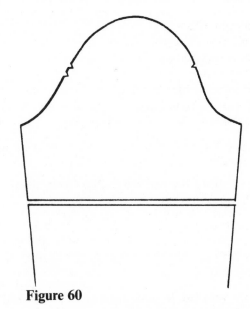

Figure 60

Figure 61

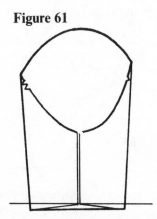

Figure 62

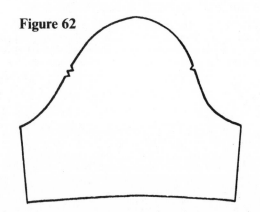

DESIGNING THE PATTERN

Flare can be given to a short sleeve as shown in *Figure 63*. If taken into a band, *Figure 64*, this shape gives a low puff.

For a high puff, cut the pattern (not below the notches) and spread the pieces as in *Figure 65*, reducing the hemline width, by overlapping, to your arm girth measurement plus 1 cm. The sleevehead line should be raised by 3 or 4 cm.

For a sleeve with more height or breadth in the crown, the pattern can be altered as shown in the photograph on page 45.

1 Cut to the required length and cut the hemline curve. Divide the sleevehead into sections as shown.

2 Cut out and spread the sleevehead pieces, adding 5 cm or even more to the height. (Number the pieces – they are easy to confuse.)

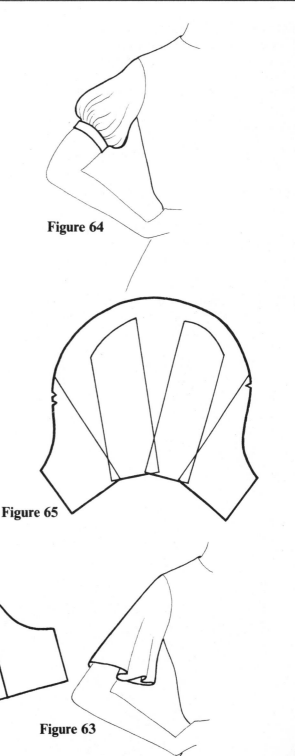

Figure 64

Figure 65

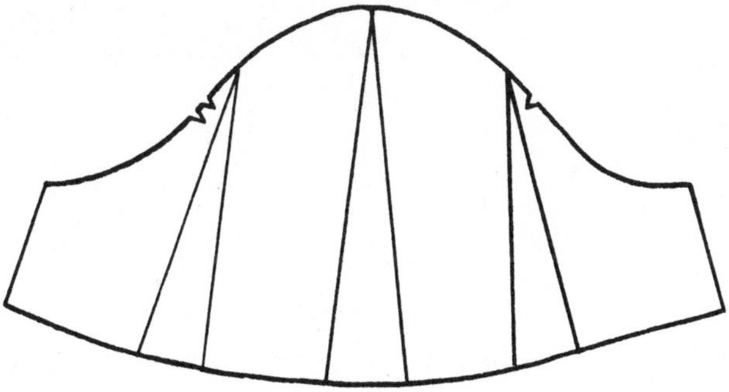

Figure 63

3 On fresh paper, draw in the new outline. This design will have four pleats; they taper like darts, but will not be stitched for their full length.

Semi-fitted sleeves

For a more fitting sleeve, an elbow dart is used, as in *Figure 66*.

1 Trace the outline of the block and cut it out. Cut along the elbow line (S to T, *Figure 21*) and cut up the two crease lines.

2 Swing the two sections of sleeve inwards, overlapping their lower ends and opening up a dart at S. The wrist measurement can be reduced by 6 or 7 cm; more if you plan a wrist opening.

3 Draw in the new outline and mark in the dart, shortened as shown to the back-arm line.

Classic shirt with wide collar

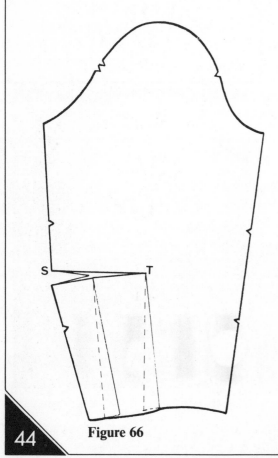

Figure 66

Full sleeves

A sleeve to be fully gathered into the armhole and into a cuff can be widened simply by cutting and spreading the pattern (*Figure 67*). Do not add any fullness outside the armhole notches.

A sleeve with fullness at the crown only is made exactly as is shown in the pattern below for a short sleeve. The fullness can be gathered in rather than pleated if you wish.

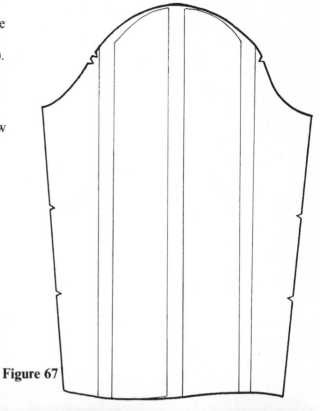

Figure 67

Pattern for a pleated sleevehead

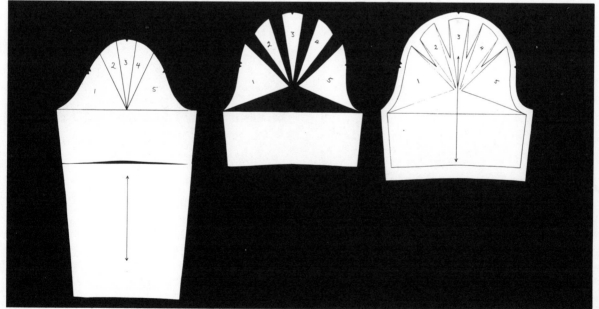

DESIGNING THE PATTERN

A sleeve with fullness below the elbow only is drafted as shown in *Figure 68*. The pattern is the same whether the sleeve is to hang loose or to be gathered into a cuff.

Wrist finishes

The simplest finish is with a casing for elastic. No alteration to the block pattern is needed (*Figure 69*).

Figure 68

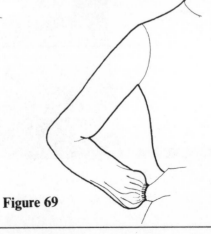

Jersey shirt with epaulets

Figure 69

A frill below the casing needs the addition of 5 cm or more to the length of the sleeve, as in the blouse on page 28.

The usual shirt-sleeve finish is with an opening and a cuff. Mark the position for the opening, 6–8 cm long, up the back crease of the sleeve pattern (*Figure 70*). Cut the cuff as a rectangle, the length of your wrist girth plus 5 cm (2 cm for ease, and 3 cm for the overlap which should be marked with a notch).

The depth of the cuff could be between 5 and 8 cm. Shorten the sleeve by the same amount.

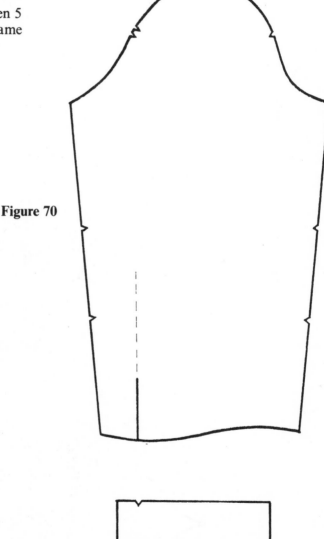

Figure 70

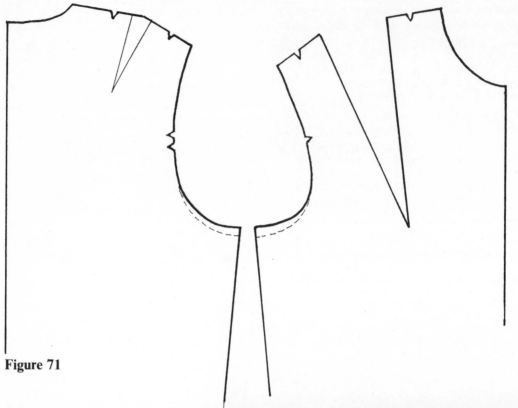

Figure 71

Blouse with slashed opening and tie neck

Sleeveless styles

A sleeveless style will need a slightly tightened armhole. The front and back blocks are cut 1·5 cm higher at the armhole curve (*Figure 71*). Cut facings 5 cm wide to finish the armholes (*Figure 72*).

Epaulets

These are taken into the shoulder seam and buttoned at the inner end – see the shirt on page 46. The epaulet should be short enough just to clear the collar, and 4–5 cm wide.

POCKETS

The proportion of the pocket to the figure, and the level at which it is applied, are both important to the finished look of the shirt.

Patch pockets need not be rectangular; their lower edge could be cut to a point – as in the photograph on page 46 – or their corners rounded. Cut the draft pocket to its finished size. Place it on the shirt pattern and draw round it to mark the final position.

A pocket in a yoke seam shows simply as a slit. Add the pocket shape to both bodice pieces, as shown in *Figure 73*. Do not make the pocket mouth wider than 8 cm, or it may gape.

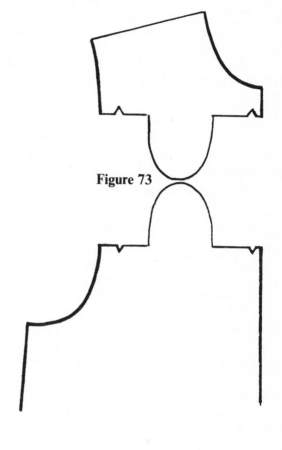

Figure 73

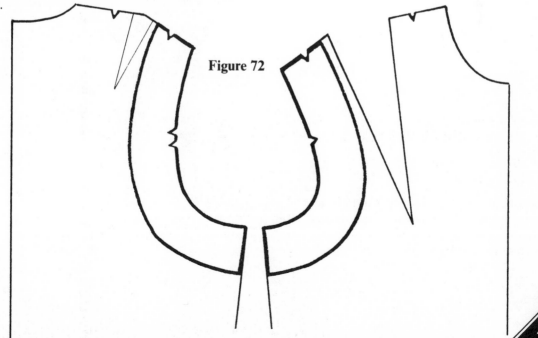

Figure 72

DESIGNING THE PATTERN

LENGTH AND HEM FINISH

Most shirts and blouses will be finished at hip level, as in the block. But if you want a short blouse with a drawstring waist or pleating into a band, then cut the bodice patterns to the waist length plus 5 cm for blousing (*Figure 74*).

A waistband should be cut to your waist measurement (plus any overlap for buttoning).

A blouse with a shirred waistline needs a further 5 cm for the depth of the shirring.

SEAM AND HEM ALLOWANCES

The pattern has been drafted 'net', without any turnings. The edges of the pattern pieces all coincide with seamlines or with the length of a finished edge. Now, with all the pieces drafted, is the time to add seam and hem allowances as in the photograph on page 45.

1 Add 1·5 cm to:
all seamlines, including the neck edge;
the edges of collar, yoke, cuffs and waistband;
pocket edges. (Add 2·5 cm to the opening edge of a patch pocket, to act as a facing.)

2 To the hem edge add:
2·5 cm for a normal hem;
2·5 cm for a drawstring casing;
1·5 cm if the waist is to be set into a band;
5 cm as a facing if the waist is to be shirred.

3 To sleeve edges add:
1·5 cm for setting into a cuff;
2·5 cm for an elastic casing;
2·5 cm for a normal hem;
1 cm only for narrow hem on fully flared sleeve.

4 No seam allowances are needed along the free edges of facings.

Draw or rule at these distances outside all the pattern outlines and cut out. Mark notches along the new edges. Check that the names of the pieces and straight-grain lines or fold-arrows are marked on all of them.

These are the final patterns ready for laying out on the fabric.

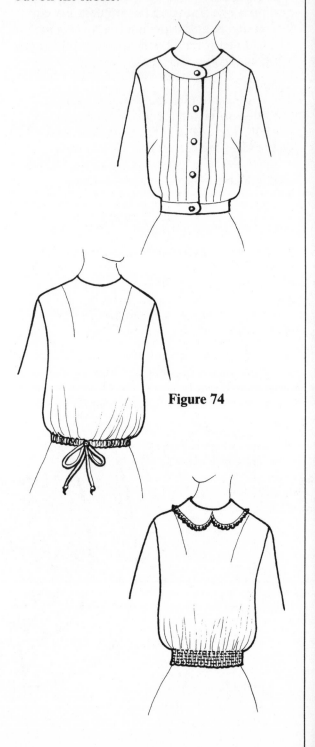

Figure 74

DESIGNING THE PATTERN

FABRIC REQUIREMENTS

As you are not working with a commercial pattern you will not have the guidance, given on the pattern envelope, as to the length of fabric needed. So first choose your fabric, note its width and also any check or one-way design that may have to be matched. Next, make a pattern layout to see how much material you will need to buy. Only after you have done all this should you buy your fabric.

The pattern layout

Unless you have a really large table, plan the layout of the pattern pieces on the floor.

1 Take the width of the fabric when folded in half, with the selvages matched. Use the edge of a carpet to represent the fold of the fabric, and a long ruler or straight edge, placed parallel to it and the appropriate distance away, to represent the selvage edges.

2 Place your pattern pieces, as economically as possible, with the straight-grain arrows parallel to the edges and fold-arrows placed to the fold. *Figure 75* shows a typical layout: lay the larger pieces first, and the smaller ones where they will fit.

3 Check the number of pattern pieces you will need. As your fabric will be folded, you will automatically cut two of each piece. But you will need four pieces for cuffs or for a lined yoke, so patterns for these will have to be cut twice over.

4 If you have chosen a fabric with a one-way design or surface texture, then all the pattern pieces must be laid with their tops towards the same end of the layout.

5 If the fabric is checked, add one complete repeat of the check to the measured length of your layout to allow precise matching.

The fabric and notions

Only now are you ready to calculate the length needed, and to buy the fabric. At the same time, buy what Americans call the 'notions' – the necessary bits and pieces to make up the garment:
matching thread and if necessary buttonhole twist for top-stitching;
plastic neckline zip;
buttons;
bias binding for casings and collar edges;
interfacing for collar, cuffs and facings (non-woven interfacings are usually too stiff for collars, though the lighter weight is suitable for cuffs. A plain white polyester-cotton makes a good general-purpose interfacing that washes well).

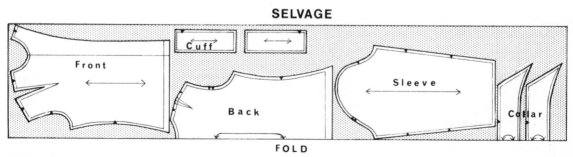

SELVAGE

FOLD

Figure 75

MAKING UP THE BLOUSE

From here onwards, all is straightforward. The instructions that follow give the sequence in which you should work, whatever type of blouse or shirt you are making. As you go along, pick out the instructions for your particular design and disregard the rest.

The methods given are easy and can be applied to almost any design. If you are a seasoned dressmaker, you may find the instructions unnecessarily detailed; you may in any case prefer another way of setting on a collar, for instance, or choose to dispense with some facings. So please skip what you do not need.

CUTTING OUT
Fold the fabric lengthwise, with the right side inside. It is important that the selvages be perfectly matched, so that the fold is exactly on the straight grain of the fabric.

Place the pattern pieces in the positions you have planned, with their straight-grain arrows parallel to the selvages. A fold-arrow goes precisely to the fold, not a millimetre or two away from it. With a checked fabric, the most conspicuous line – or the centre of the space between checks – should come at the centre-front and back.

Smooth the pieces down their centres, hold them with one pin at each end, check the straight-grain arrow again, and then smooth out and pin down the corners. Finally, pin all round the piece at intervals of 10–15 cm.

When you cut out, notches should be cut outwards, not into the seam allowances. Leave the patterns pinned to blouse pieces.

Cut interfacings to correspond to cuff, collar and facings, and to the same pattern. Front facings cut in one with the blouse front are interfaced as far as the fold.

MARKING
The patterns already have their seam allowances marked round the fitting lines. It is extremely important that your seams be stitched precisely along these lines, or the fit will be affected. So mark the vital points through the pattern on to the fabric, as a guide for your machining. There are several ways to do this.

Dressmaker's carbon paper
Insert the carbon paper (face downwards) between the pattern and the upper layer of fabric; place another carbon (face upwards) under the lower layer. On a firm surface, mark through the pattern with the tracing wheel, making a cross at the point to be marked. The marks will be transferred to the wrong side of the fabric.

Tailor's tacks
This method is nearly as quick, and rather more reliable since carbon markings may not show up well on prints.

1 Using a double thread, take a tiny stitch through the pattern and both thicknesses of fabric, at the point to be marked (*Figure 76*).

2 Take another stitch through the same point, and leave a loop big enough to put your finger through (*Figure 77*).

3 Cut the thread, leaving 1 cm ends (*Figure 78*).

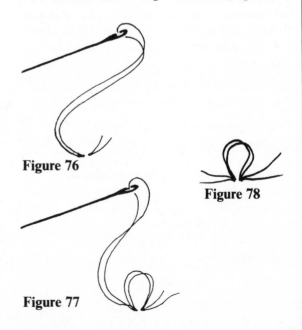

Figure 76

Figure 78

Figure 77

4 When you have marked all the points on the pattern piece, gently tear off the pattern. If your stitches were small, so will the holes be. Then ease apart the two layers of fabric, and cut the threads between them (*Figure 79*).

5 You will be left with tufts of thread in each piece of fabric which can be matched with their opposite numbers when you pin the seams.

Points to be marked

1 The points where seamlines cross, such as the ends of a yoke, and the underarm points of bodice and sleeve.

2 Dart markings, at the the seamline and at the point.

3 Pleat markings, at the fold and the stitching lines. Mark at intervals down the blouse, to ensure the accuracy of your tacking and pressing. Tuck markings, at the top and bottom of the tucks.

4 The corners of patch pocket placings.

5 The positions of buttons and buttonholes.

FITTING

Even though the pattern has been cut to your own measurements, the fitting of the blouse on the figure is important for a smooth line. Get a friend to help you – it is next to impossible to make alterations on yourself.

Tack the back and front darts, then tack the shoulder and side seams. Try on the blouse – it should hang smoothly from the shoulders.

1 Check first the fit round the neck, remembering that the finished neckline will fall 1·5 cm lower than the raw edges. Any adjustment, such as a slight raising or lowering of the line round the neck, will also affect the collar and facings. However, such an alteration would be small and quite manageable within the existing seam allowances.

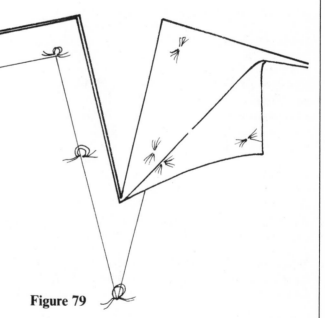

Figure 79

2 Now look at the darts – are they the right length? The length of the darts can be adjusted if necessary, but not their width at the seamline. Shortening a dart will add width at its point, and vice versa.

3 Next check the slope of the shoulders. If your shoulders are square, you may find creases pulling downwards from the point of the shoulder (*Figure 80*). To correct this, let out the shoulder seam a little towards the armhole end, and re-tack it with narrower seam turnings. Do not alter the neck end of the seam.

If your shoulders are sloping, you may see a fold drooping from the neck to below the shoulder (*Figure 81*). The remedy is to lift the blouse at the shoulder, and re-tack the seam to take in slightly wider turnings towards the armhole end. If this makes the armhole too tight, trim up to 1 cm from its lower edge under the arm.

4 Check the length of the shoulder seam: the sleeve seam should cross it at the point of the shoulder, where you can feel the bone. Mark this point if necessary, so that you can set in the sleeve at that level. However, a blouse should have an easy fit – do not make the shoulders narrower unless you are quite sure the alteration is necessary.

5 If you want back and front waist darts, pin them in now. They should be centred down the line L–Q on the back pattern (*Figure 19*) and X–S on the front (*Figure 20*). Pin them as needed on your figure, widest at the waistline and tapering to nothing below the bust and above the hemline.

6 If you have made any substantial alterations, mark them also on the back and front blocks, for future use. Then you should not again have to spend time on fitting.

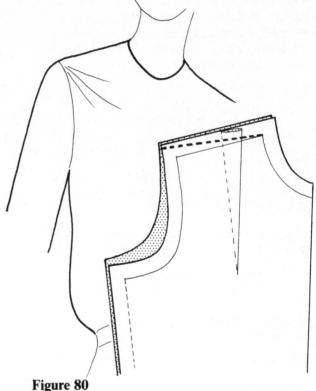

Figure 80

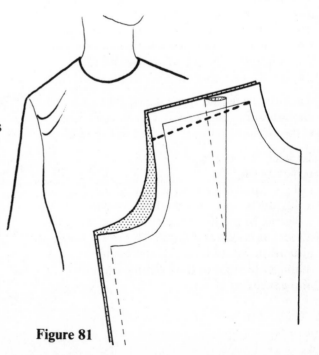

Figure 81

MAKING UP THE BLOUSE

DARTS

Stitch the darts first, from wide end to point. Press them towards the centre; side and sleeve darts are pressed downwards. The point of the dart should be finely tapered off.

YOKES

1 Gather, pleat or tuck the bodice section to fit the yoke.

2 Pleats should be tacked for their whole length, and stitched down for a few centimetres below the yoke if liked. Tucks should be stitched for their whole length and pressed outwards from the centre.

For gathering, use the longest machine stitch. Work two rows of gathers, 1 cm and again 2 cm from the edge. Pull up the gathering threads to fit.

3 With right sides together, and matching the notches, stitch the yoke to the lower section. (With gathers, remove the gathering thread that shows.)

4 For a yoke pocket, stitch one end of the yoke seam, then round the pocket bag, then the other end of the yoke seam, all in one operation (*Figure 82*).

Shaped yokes, especially if they have corners, are better top-stitched in place. Clip and press under the seam allowances of the yoke. With right sides upwards, tack and top-stitch the yoke over the lower section, close to the folded edge (*Figure 83*).

FINISHING RAW EDGES

Finish yoke seams by working zigzag machine stitching (or hand overcasting) over both raw edges together. Press the turnings upwards towards the yoke.

Turnings of shoulder, side and sleeve seams should be pressed apart, their edges creased under narrowly, and machine-stitched as shown in *Figure 84*.

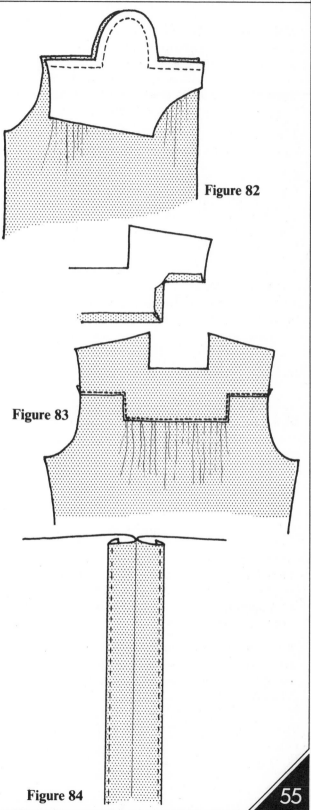

Figure 82

Figure 83

Figure 84

THE NECKLINE ZIP

Zip-fasteners (US zipper) are set in before the neck finish is worked, so that the ends of the tapes can later be taken into the neckline seam. Zips are much easier to set into flat fabric, before the side seams are stitched.

1 First stitch the seam up to the bottom end of the zip placing.

2 With the longest machine stitch, baste together the sides of the opening up to the neckline. Press the edges open.

3 Centre the zip under the basted opening. Pin and tack it in place.

4 Use a piping or zipper foot on the machine to allow stitching close to the zipper chain, along the centre of the tapes. From the wrong side, stitch as shown in *Figure 85*, down one side, across the bottom and up the other side.

5 Remove the basting threads.

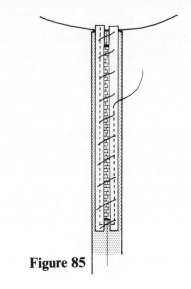

Figure 85

THE SEAMS

Stitch and finish the shoulder and side seams.

COLLARS

Make up the collar, including the interfacing.

1 Place the two layers of collar right sides together, with the interfacing on top. Tack and stitch the outer edges.

2 Trim the seam turnings in layers, clip curves and trim the points as shown in *Figure 86*.

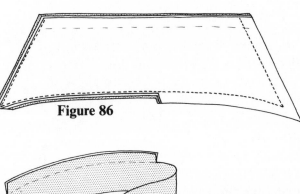

Figure 86

3 Turn right side out and press, so that the seam falls a hair's breadth to the underside of the collar.

4 Top-stitch round the collar edge, if liked, with a long machine stitch.

Make up a tie collar (as in *Figure 54*) by stitching along the ends and the long edge, and leaving at the centre a gap the length of the neckline. Turn right side out and clip the turnings at the ends of the opening. Stitch these turnings only into the neckline seam (*Figure 87*).

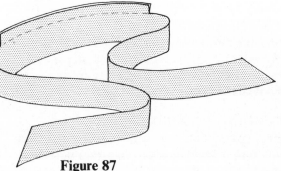

Figure 87

FACINGS

With or without a collar, you will have neckline facings and their corresponding interfacings.

1 Tack the interfacings to the wrong side of the facings.

2 Stitch the back and front facings together at the shoulder seams. Press the seams open and trim the interfacing edges close to the seamline.

3 Finish the free edge of facing and interfacing together with zigzag stitching.

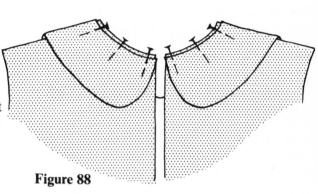

Figure 88

For a blouse with a back opening

1 Pin any collar in place round the outside of the neckline (*Figure 88*). Match the collar notches to the shoulder seams, and the ends of the collar to the centre-back. (The bodice neckline will appear too short for a straight-cut collar, but if you clip it at intervals you will find that it fits along the seamline.)

2 Place the facings right side down on top, matching the shoulder seams. Fold over the ends of the facings level with the back opening. Tack all round the neckline (*Figure 89*).

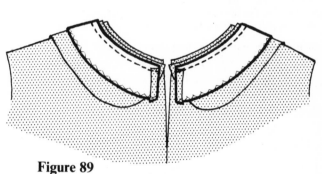

Figure 89

3 Stitch where you have tacked.

4 For a blouse *without* a collar, open out the facings and under-stitch them to the seam turnings close to the neck seam. This prevents the neckline from rolling over to expose the seam (*Figure 90*).

5 Trim and clip the seam turnings.

6 Press the facing to the inside and catch it down with a few stitches to the shoulder seam turnings.

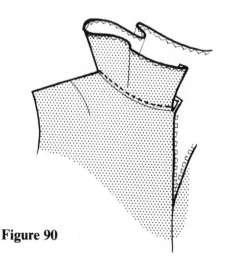

Figure 90

7 Hem the folded ends of the facing to the sides of the opening (*Figure 91*).

8 Close the top of the opening with a hook and eye – whether or not you have inserted a zip.

For a shirt with separate front facings
1 Tack the collar round the neckline, as before, matching the notches to the shoulder seams and the ends of the collar to the centre-front marking.

2 Tack the facings (right sides together) to the fronts and round the neck (*Figure 92*). Stitch as one seam right round, including the lower ends of the facings along the hemline.

3 Clip and trim the turnings.

4 Turn the facings to the inside, and press.

For a shirt with attached front facings
The procedure is exactly as above, except that the facings seam will be round the neckline only (*Figure 93*). The front edges of the shirt will be folded, not seamed.

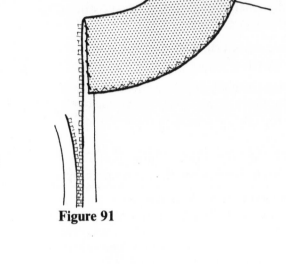

Figure 91

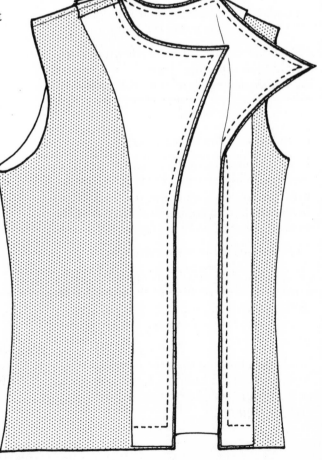

Figure 92

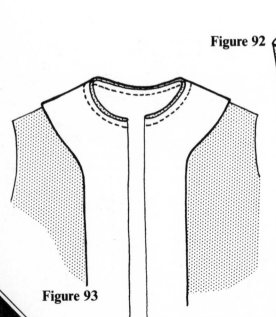

Figure 93

MAKING UP THE BLOUSE

For right-side facings
Blouses like the one shown at the bottom left of *Figure 23* have their facings turned out to the right side.

1 Stitch the neck seam with the right side of the facings to the *wrong* side of the neckline.

2 Press under the raw edges round the facing.

3 Turn the facing to the outside of the blouse and top-stitch (*Figure 94*).

Armhole facings for sleeveless styles
Tack the facings to their interfacings and seam them together at the shoulder and underarm seams. (Any alteration you have made to the armhole should also be made to the facings.) Finish the free edge with zigzag stitching. With right sides together, stitch the facings to the blouse armhole (*Figure 95*). Under-stitch as for neckline facings, clip the turnings and press the facings to the inside.

NECKLINES WITHOUT FACINGS

Round or scooped necklines
As in the top sketch of *Figure 23*, a round neck can be finished with bias binding.

First, prevent any stretching by machining round the neckline 2 cm from the edge. Trim off the 1·5 cm seam allowance.

With right sides together, stitch one crease of the binding to the neckline. Turn the free edge of the binding to the inside and hem the fold to the previous stitching (*Figure 96*).

Necklines gathered with casings for elastic
A neckline like that in *Figure 37* is also finished with bias binding.

Turn the neckline seam allowances to the wrong side, clipping curves if necessary, and press.

Stitch bias binding over the turnings, close to both folds of the binding. Leave a short gap in the lower row of stitching to thread in the elastic (*Figure 97*).

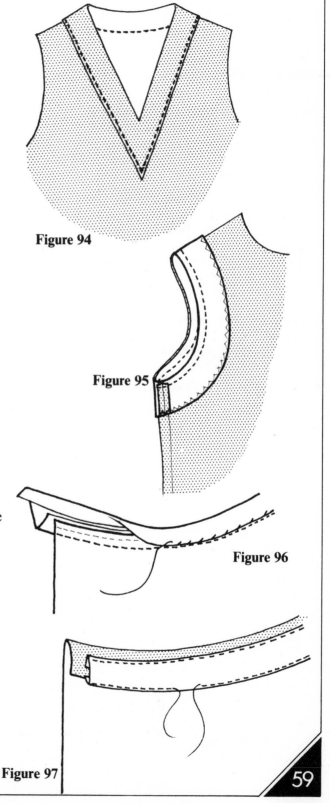

Figure 94

Figure 95

Figure 96

Figure 97

MAKING UP THE BLOUSE

SLEEVES

First make up and finish the sleeves; then set them into the armholes.

Sleeve openings

A cuff will need a sleeve opening above it. Work this before the sleeve seam.

1 Machine up one side of the marked opening, and down the other. Take one stitch across the point. Cut up to the point of the opening (*Figure 98*).

2 Cut a strip of fabric twice the length of the opening, by 3 cm wide. Tack it to the right side of the opening. With the sleeve uppermost, stitch 0·5 cm from the edge of the strip (*Figure 99*). At the middle you will be stitching only a thread or two away from the point of the opening.

3 Turn the strip to the wrong side of the sleeve, fold in 0·5 cm along its edge and hem to the previous stitching (*Figure 100*). Press towards the front of the sleeve.

4 Now stitch and finish the sleeve seam.

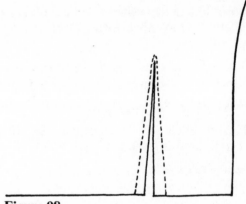

Figure 98

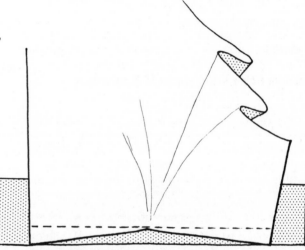

Figure 99

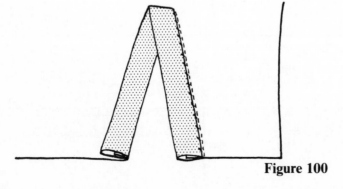

Figure 100

Cuffs

Make up a cuff like a collar, with right sides together, and the interfacing on top.

1 Stitch round the side and bottom edges, and along the top edge of the buttoning extension (*Figure 101*).

2 Trim and clip the turnings, turn right side out and press.

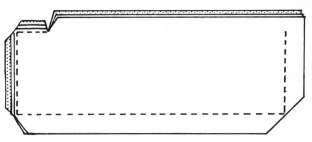

Figure 101

3 Top-stitch round the cuff edge if liked, with a long machine stitch.

4 Pleat or gather the sleeve to fit the cuff. With right sides together, stitch the sleeve to the cuff and interfacing (not to the inner layer of the cuff). The buttoning extension goes to the back edge of the sleeve.

5 Turn in and hem the cuff facing to the seamline (*Figure 102*).

Epaulets

Stitch round the sides and pointed end. Trim, turn right side out, press and top-stitch if liked. Tack to the shirt over the shoulder seam. The unfinished end is taken into the armhole seam.

Hemmed sleeves

Turn up a 2·5 cm hem, fold in the raw edge and slip-hem (*Figure 103*). For a widely-flared sleeve, a very narrow hem, not more than 1 cm wide, will set better round the curved edge.

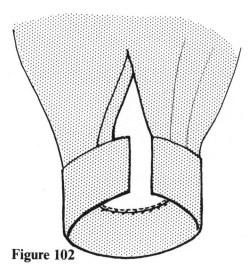

Figure 102

Wrist casings for elastic

Work these as for neckline casings. If you want a frill below the elastic, as in the photograph on page 28, finish the edge with a very narrow machined hem, and set the casing 3–5 cm higher on the wrong side.

Short sleeve band

For a sleeve such as the one shown in *Figure 64*, interface the band and stitch its seam. Gather the sleeve edge to fit the band. With the right sides together, stitch the band to the sleeve, fold in the free edge and hem it to the seamline on the wrong side.

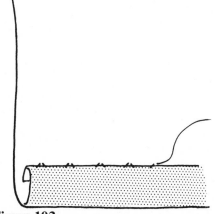

Figure 103

MAKING UP THE BLOUSE

Setting in the sleeves

1 Gather the sleevehead between the notches.

2 Turn the blouse inside out. Put the sleeve (right side out) inside the blouse, matching the underarm seams. Check by the notches that you have the sleeve in its proper armhole – the double notch identifies the back edge (*Figure 104*).

3 Pin together from the underarm seam up to the notches.

4 Pin the centre of the sleevehead to the shoulder seam. Spread the gathers to fit and pin.

5 Tack and then remove the pins.

6 Try on the blouse. The sleeve should hang without wrinkles. If there are any creases pulling from the front of the armhole, and loose folds at the back, as in *Figure 105*, move the sleevehead gathers slightly towards the front of the armhole. If the creases pull from behind the shoulder and there are loose folds in front, as in *Figure 106*, then move the gathers slightly towards the back of the armhole. Tack the altered position.

7 Stitch the armhole seam. Stitch again 0·5 cm inside the seam allowance, trim almost to the second row of machining, and finish with zigzag stitching over the edge.

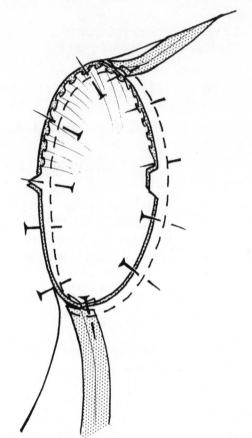

Figure 104

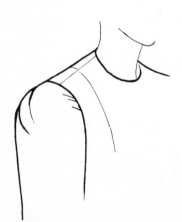

Figure 105

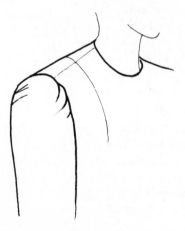

Figure 106

POCKETS

1 Turn under 0·5 cm along the pocket facing edge and machine.

2 Turn the pocket facing to the *right* side. Stitch the short seam at each end, and stitch round the pocket bag on the fitting line (*Figure 107*).

3 Turn the pocket facing over to the inside. Press under the turnings along the stitched line. Fold in the corners (*Figure 108*).

4 Match the pocket exactly to its marked position on the blouse, and top-stitch in place. Begin and end with a small triangle of stitching, for strength (*Figure 109*).

THE WAIST FINISH

Hems

The pattern allows for a plain hem 2·5 cm deep. Work this by hand or machine.

For a front-buttoned shirt, turn up the hem first, and let the facings cover the hem ends (*Figure 110*).

Waistline casing for drawstring

Turn up the hem to form the casing. Make a small buttonhole at the centre-front to thread in the drawstring. Stitch the casing along its upper and lower edges – see the centre sketch of *Figure 74*.

Waistband

This is set on in exactly the same way as a cuff is set on to a sleeve. The waistline will need to be gathered first. The buttoning extension is set to the right-hand side of the bodice as shown in *Figure 74*.

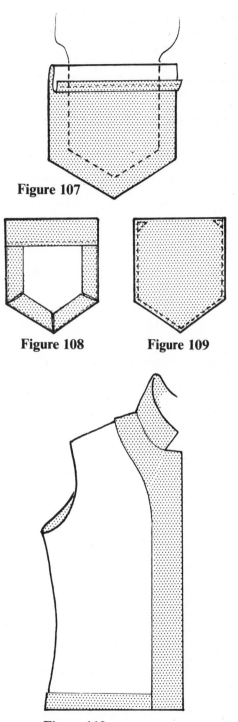

Figure 107

Figure 108   **Figure 109**

Figure 110

Shirred waistline

The lowest sketch of *Figure 74* shows the effect of a shirred waist.

1 Neaten the raw edge with zigzag stitching.

2 Tack up a 5 cm hem turning.

3 Wind the bobbin of the machine with shirring elastic; do not change the needle-thread. Set the longest machine stitch.

4 Beginning at a side seam, and working with the right side up, stitch right round the wastline 1 cm from the edge of the hem.

5 Work four more rows, each a scant centimetre above the last (*Figure 111*).

6 If the shirring gives too slack a fit to the waist, pull up the ends of the elastic more tightly. Pull the needle-threads through to the wrong side, and knot the ends very firmly, row by row.

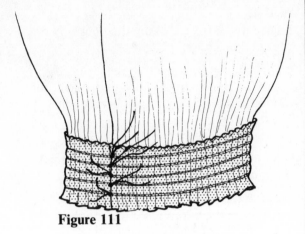

Figure 111

BUTTONS AND BUTTONHOLES

Down the right front of the blouse and on the front edges of cuffs, make hand-worked or preferably machine-worked buttonholes. (Machines vary: follow the instruction booklet for your own machine.)

Measure and mark the length and spacing of the buttonholes.

For small shirt buttons, the buttonholes should be vertical; for larger buttons, it is better to set them horizontally.

Sew buttons to the left front and to the cuffs, to correspond with the buttonholes.